THE LITTLE GUIDE TO
PRADA

First published in 2025 by OH
An Imprint of HEADLINE PUBLISHING GROUP LIMITED

1

Disclaimer:

Cataloguing in Publication Data is available from the British Library

ISBN 978-1-03542-239-5

Compiled and written by: Katie Meegan
Editorial: Saneaah Muhammad
Designed and typeset in Avenir by: Stephen Cary
Project manager: Russell Porter
Production: Arlene Lestrade
Printed and bound in China

MIX
Paper | Supporting
responsible forestry
FSC® C104740
www.fsc.org

HEADLINE PUBLISHING GROUP LIMITED
An Hachette UK Company
Carmelite House, 50 Victoria Embankment, London EC4Y 0DZ

The authorised representative in the EEA is Hachette Ireland, 8 Castlecourt Centre, Castleknock Road, Castleknock, Dublin 15, D15 YF6A, Ireland

www.headline.co.uk   www.hachette.co.uk

THE LITTLE GUIDE TO

PRADA

STYLE TO LIVE BY

Unofficial and Unauthorized

CONTENTS

INTRODUCTION

It's hard to believe that a fashion house so forward-thinking and innovative could be over a century old. Prada, helmed by the world-renowned Miuccia Prada, has been changing how we view luxury, elegance and – by extension – ourselves since the 1980s. More than handbags and high fashion, Prada's influence extends far beyond the catwalk into art, film, theatre and even to how we shop.

Founded in 1913 by brothers Mario and Martino Prada, the leather-goods designer was the epitome of bourgeois luxury. Although Prada remained a coveted brand throughout the twentieth century, it was Miuccia Prada, along with her husband and business partner Patrizio Bertelli, that turned this Milanese leather shop into the cultural behemoth it is today.

An initially reluctant heir to the Prada name, Miuccia Prada has set the bar for the fashion industry for nearly five decades. Prada's innovative use of once-overlooked materials, such as military-grade nylon, single-handedly transformed how we view materials and, by extension, how we define luxury.

The iconic nylon backpack, for example, epitomizes the unique Prada blend of practicality and sophistication, a philosophy extends to Prada's intellectual runway designs, where each collection is a thoughtful amalgamation of art and culture, and a commentary on contemporary life.

It could be said that the true innovative spirit of Prada lies in tension. Tension between Miuccia Prada's early political affiliations with leftist politics and her inherited love of fashion; tension between high art and esoteric concepts and yearning for functionality; tension between how we define beauty and how we define fashion itself. This little book is a tantalizing glimpse into the exclusive, complicated and luxurious world of Prada.

CHAPTER
ONE

THE ORIGINS
OF PRADA

FROM A MILANESE LEATHER-
GOODS SHOP TO BECOMING
THE OFFICIAL SUPPLIER OF THE
ITALIAN ROYAL FAMILY AND
MOVING ON TO THE INNOVATION
OF THE 1980s, PRADA'S UNIQUE
RISE TO GLOBAL PROMINENCE
IS SOMETHING TO BEHOLD.

Prada was founded in 1913 by brothers Mario and Martino Prada. Named Fratelli Prada (Prada Brothers), their first leather-goods shop was located in the prestigious Galleria Vittorio Emanuele II in Milan, where it is still housed today.

[Prada is a] constant fusion
of traditional values and
techniques with ground-breaking
modern ideas.

Laia Farran Graves

The Little Book of Prada, Carlton Books, 2012

The brothers sold bags, trucks and travel accessories, specializing in luxury ocean travel, which was common at the time.

The brothers quickly became known for their fine craftsmanship.

Milano da 1913.

The inscription that can be found on every metal
Prada triangle logo.

In 1919, their status as the go-to destination for the upper-middle classes was cemented when the Italian royal household named Prada as their official supplier.

Precise, direct, meaningful,
it is a shape that resonates without
words.

The words of Prada themselves on the power of their logo,
pradagroup.com, May 12, 2022

This honour meant that Prada was allowed to display the House of Savoy coat of arms and knotted rope design in its trademark triangular logo.

The logo remains the same to this day.

The Prada brothers
remained at the helm of the
brand until they retired
in 1958.

It was up to Mario Prada,
the only brother to
have children, to name
a successor.

Mario Prada, a traditionalist, believed that women had no place in business.

Mario attempted to pass the business to his son, who held no interest in managing the brand.

Eventually, despite his previous beliefs, Mario handed the business to his youngest daughter, Luisa.

Under Luisa's steady guidance, Prada continued to produce fine leather goods and upscale accessories.

Throughout the subsequent 20 years, the brand transitioned from a focus on ocean-liner travel to the increasingly popular air travel.

"

If Harvard was a billionaire woman, it would be Miuccia Prada.

"

Francesco Vezzoli

Italian artist Francesco Vezzoli, a close friend of Miuccia Prada, *New York Times Style Magazine*, October 22, 2023

By the end of Luisa's reign, the business was reporting annual sales of $450,000.

Like her father before her, Luisa turned to her daughter, Miuccia, to take over the family business.

The heir to the family business, Miuccia Prada was born Maria Bianchi Prada on May 10, 1949, in Milan, Italy, to Luisa Prada and Luigi "Gino" Bianchi.

The second of three children, she is Mario Prada's youngest granddaughter.

Even now, my mother will grab a dress I make and rub it and say, 'This silk is horrible. It's nothing your grandfather would even have been willing to sell. Can't you do better than this?'

Miuccia Prada

On her mother, Luisa Prada, newyorker.com, March 7, 2004

When I was young, I always wanted to be different.

Miuccia Prada

Vogue.com, February 13, 2024

Not only were the family affluent from her mother's Prada side, but Miuccia's father, Gino Bianchi, also owned his own successful business – manufacturing putting-green mowers.

Then [when I was 15] I started really having fun. I was out, out, out.
I remember turning my skirt into a mini-skirt on the stairs before going to school and taking it down again before coming back.

Miuccia Prada

Remembering her youth in Milan, anothermag.com, December 10, 2018

I was always frustrated, because
I had to dress so seriously. I was
a proper young girl, and I was
dreaming of pink shoes, red shoes,
pink dresses. Anything with colour.
Exciting underwear. Everybody
had this kind of dull underwear and
wore boring striped dresses.
I couldn't stand it.

Miuccia Prada

On chafing against what was fashionable at the time,
newyorker.com, March 7, 2004

As with well-to-do families of the time, Miuccia attended an all-girls Catholic school, where she showed great aptitude and intelligence.

Far from the world of fashion that she would become synonymous with, Miuccia attended the University of Milan, where she studied Political Science.

Throughout her time as a student, her political views became increasingly feminist and left-wing.

The biggest change in my life happened when I went from being a Catholic bourgeois to a left-wing activist.

Miuccia Prada

On her introduction to politics, wmagazine.com, December 11, 2015

In the 1970s, Miuccia became an active member of the Italian Communist party, often attending events and protests.

However, she often felt conflicted between her strong political views and her love of fashion, which she felt were at odds with each other.

I hated the bourgeois people who felt they had to dress in jeans when you knew they didn't want to.

Miuccia Prada

On her student style; she is reported to have worn Yves Saint Laurent to student protests, newyorker.com, March 7, 2004

I used to wear Saint Laurent all the time. I always liked the bourgeoisie. I was intrigued by the bourgeoisie. But mainly that was the culture of the 60s and 70s.

Miuccia Prada

On the tension between her style and her political beliefs, anothermag.com, December 10, 2018

I was so embarrassed when I was young. To be a leftist feminist and doing fashion, I felt so horrible and so ashamed.

Miuccia Prada

The sentiment that Miuccia Prada often returns to: her inner conflict between politics and fashion, vanityfair.com, August 1, 2019

I really believed we could transform the world.

Miuccia Prada

On her idealistic student years, *New York Times Style Magazine*, October 22, 2023

Doing clothes [while coming from] a group of very important intellectuals – for me it was like a nightmare. I was so ashamed, but anyway I did it.

Miuccia Prada

On being torn between intellectualism and design, vogue.com, February 12, 2024

Despite her ongoing internal conflict, as well as pressure to join the family business, Miuccia graduated in 1973 with a PhD in Political Science from the University of Milan.

However, her burgeoning political career took an unexpected turn when she began training as a mime in Milan's Piccolo Teatro.

I attended mime lessons at the Piccolo Teatro in Milan in order to find the 'unknown' and the 'new'.

Miuccia Prada

On the decision to become a mime, wmagazine.com, December 11, 2015

Fashion critics, and Miuccia herself, have noted the "embodied" nature of Prada's design.

In a podcast interview with Vogue in 2022, she admitted that the way in which she constructs movement into clothing may have been inspired by her time as a mime.

I got very serious, and I was a really good mime – especially when it was abstract. It's fun controlling your body. I was curious about so many things.

Miuccia Prada

Reminiscing on her five-year-long career as a mime, newyorker.com, March 7, 2004

> "
>
> This is conjecture, but seeing as Mrs Prada studied to be a mime, I think you need to work harder in her clothes… You have to work for it, you have to interpret what the message is.
>
> "

Laird Borrelli-Persson

Vogue Archive Editor, *Vogue: The Archives* podcast, Episode 5, "Prada: A Revolution From Within", November 2, 2022

Miuccia's dreams of mime came to an abrupt ending five years later, when her parents forbade her to continue in the theatre.

Instead she turned her attention toward the family business.

However, the "frivolity" of fashion continued to clash with her feminist ideologies.

I always thought there were only two noble professions: politicians or doctors.

Miuccia Prada

On her ambitions to be a politician before joining her family's business, vogue.com, February 12, 2024

Now, I'm not saying I'm fashionable, but there are sociological interests that matter to me, things that are theoretical, political, intellectual and also concerned with vanity and beauty that we all think about, but that I try to mix up and translate into fashion.

Miuccia Prada

On the meeting point between politics and fashion, vogue.com, September 24, 2021

Eventually, after taking over the Prada brand, Miuccia discovered how to meld her politics with fashion and, in turn, created one of the most forward-thinking fashion houses of the latter half of the twentieth century.

I never declare my political intention, because I think in fashion, in luxury business, it's better to shut up.

Miuccia Prada

On navigating her political views and the fashion world, vanityfair.com, August 1, 2019

Fashion is mostly loved by intellectuals and fashionistas. Much less by the bourgeoisie.

Miuccia Prada

Revealing the true devotees of fashion, wmagazine.com, December 11, 2015

Miuccia Prada's formative years in politics and the theatre can be traced throughout the following decades, through the production of "intelligent" clothes that gave rise to her title of an "intellectual designer".

CHAPTER
TWO

AN ACCESSORY REVOLUTION

PRADA WOULD SIMPLY NOT BE PRADA WITHOUT THE FAMOUS NYLON BAG. FIRST CONCEIVED IN 1979, THIS SIGNATURE BAG CHANGED HOW WE SAW TEXTILES AND, BY EXTENSION, LUXURY ITSELF.

Prada, although a prestige heritage brand, had maintained the level of interest of the early days and by the late 1970s, the brand had shrunk to one store.

Miuccia Prada took over from her mother in 1978, tasked with invigorating the now sleepy and stagnant leather-goods designer.

I wanted at first to do only bags.

Miuccia Prada

Reflecting on her early career in Prada and taking over her grandfather's leather-goods atelier, newyorker.com, March 7, 2004

In 1978 Miuccia Prada met her now-husband, and long-time collaborator, Patrizio Bertelli at a trade show, where he was a rival in the leather-goods industry.

They married the same year.

Prada credits Bertelli for pushing her to design shoes and, eventually, ready-to-wear fashion.

When she works, she is happy. When she does beautiful things, she is happy. When she travels, she is happy. When she spends time with intelligent people, she is happy.

Patrizio Bertelli

Speaking to *Vogue* about his wife, Miuccia Prada, vogue.com, February 12, 2024

He had all these ideas about what
I should do with my business. He
has been pushing me ever since.

Miuccia Prada

On her husband and business partner Patrizio Bertelli,
newyorker.com, March 7, 2004

"

Interrogation, curiosity, intellectual honesty. She may be quite a contrarian, but she has very specific historic references, and she has an understanding of costume, which is absolutely deep.

Patrizio Bertelli

On Miuccia's deep knowledge of the world, newyorker.com, March 7, 2004

Miuccia began experimenting, making waterproof backpacks out of Pocono, a nylon fabric previously used to make WWII tents.

Prada released the first set of backpacks and totes in 1979.

Success was not overnight, and the bags proved hard to sell due to high prices and a lack of advertising.

Risk is something I kind of like.

Miuccia Prada

On her departure from fashion norms, vogue.com, February 12, 2024

In 1985, as Prada began to expand again under Miuccia and Bertelli's guidance, Prada re-launched the 1979 Pocono nylon bags.

This time, with a good chain and the understated triangular Prada logo, the bags were a sensation.

Suddenly, nylon started to look more intriguing to me than couture fabrics.

Miuccia Prada

On her departure from more traditional luxury fabrics, pradagroup.com, July 21, 2023

"

Prada employed synthetics such as polyester and nylon with clean precision in their utilitarian minimalism; their simple black or navy nylon backpack became iconic of the [1990s].

"

Emmanuelle Dirix

High Fashion: The 20th Century Decade by Decade, 2015

I like to push, because in the push you become more creative, more intelligent.

Miuccia Prada

On her design ethos, vogue.com, February 12, 2024

Prada Bags
101

Throughout the following decades, Prada designs have remained at the forefront of the most covetable bags.

Often, Miuccia herself returns to the designs again and again for fresh takes and inspiration, combining history with innovation – though the key designs remain the most iconic.

Vela Backpack

Reintroduced in 2019, the updated version of the original Prada backpack is made with a new eco-friendly synthetic nylon textile named Econyl.

The style remains as iconic as ever with the double front pockets and over-the-top flap.

[Miuccia Prada] did to nylon what Gabrielle Chanel did to jersey.

Lilah Ramzi

"Prada Handbags 101", vogue.com, July 21, 2023

Re-Edition 1995

First debuted in 1995, this sleek and simple design marked a return to Prada's luxury leather roots.

An elegant yet structured bag, it is made with brushed leather, creating a glossy look.

Prada Moon

Featuring details taken from the sailing world, the Prada Moon screams Y2K style, with a puffed-up leather base mixed with the signature Prada nylon.

Re-Edition 2005

The quintessential Prada
day-to-day bag comes in
both leather and nylon and is
a staple for fashionistas and
celebrities alike.

Galleria

A relatively new addition to the Prada stable, the Galleria bag was introduced in 2007. Crafted in Saffiano leather (a material patented by Miuccia's grandfather and the founder of Prada), the bag is a nod to Prada's origins in Milan's Galleria Vittorio Emanuele II. Today, the rectangular bag consists of 83 hand-finished pieces, including two top handles and two zipper closures.

"

[Using nylon] not only revolutionized the concept of luggage itself, but more importantly it gave way to a new aesthetic of contrasting fabrics, textures and clean lines, which became very much part of the label's signature and design identity.

Laia Farran Graves

The Little Book of Prada, 2012

Cleo

Another new addition to
the Prada bag line-up is the
Cleo, which debuted
in Spring/Summer 2021.

Larger than the Re-edition
2005 but with a curved base,
the Cleo is made of luxurious
brushed calfskin and lightweight
spazzolato calf leather.

Throughout the many iterations of the Prada bag, we can see Miuccia returning to the same core tenets of practicality and beauty: an incongruous blend that she continued to push to the limits in the following decades of ready-to-wear fashion.

Nappa Antique Tote

This everyday essential was elevated by using crinkled antique leather, which is wrinkled by hand to give the tote bag it's unique appearance.

In the end, the love for objects prevailed.

Miuccia Prada

On her love of handbags, vanityfair.com, August 1, 2019

CHAPTER
THREE

MINIMALISM
vs
UGLY CHIC

WHILE IT IS DIFFICULT TO
PINPOINT EXACTLY WHAT THE
PRADA LOOK IS, THERE ARE
TWO RETURNING THEMES THAT
MIUCCIA PRADA RETURNS
TO AGAIN AND AGAIN IN
HER CATWALK COLLECTIONS:
MINIMALISM AND UGLY CHIC.

Prada launched its first ready-to-wear clothing line in 1988.

Expanding from the bags and shoes that the brand had become known for, Miuccia drew inspiration from her own wardrobe and her love of vintage styles.

I also loved uniforms, and I still
do. You can hide yourself in a
uniform; you can conceal who
you are. Sometimes I like to hide
myself behind formality. I think
it's attractive.

Miuccia Prada

On her desire to create a "uniform" for the modern woman,
newyorker.com, March 7, 2004

I started to make fashion because I couldn't find anything to wear. For years I kept on buying and wearing vintage, second-hand, and uniforms… any type of uniforms.

Miuccia Prada

On her foray into ready-to-wear fashion at the end of the 1980s, wmagazine.com, December 11, 2015

I would wear Saint Laurent, Pierre Cardin and then some strange English clothes, all in a weird way. I always had to be first. That was the most important thing.

Miuccia Prada

On her love of styling vintage clothes, newyorker.com, March 7, 2004

I tend to dress in uniform.
Most of the things that I love,
I can't wear because of my age.
Like miniskirts.

Miuccia Prada

On her love for a uniform that continued throughout the decades,
vanityfair.com, August 1, 2019

The first Prada collection, marked by dark tones, dropped waistlines and narrow belts, was a direct contrast to the opulence and maximalism that marked high fashion of the 1980s.

The understated elegance of the 1988 collection, with its clean lines and understated luxury, set the tone for following Prada collections.

[Fashion is] freedom – representing yourself. We should be able to be who we choose to be, always.

Miuccia Prada

On finding freedom, vogue.com, February 12, 2024

When everything has been done, sometimes the only possibility left to be different is the idea of the traditional and the conservative.

Miuccia Prada

On being different, anothermag.com, December 10, 2018

Fashion is a representation of
one's vision of the world.
Because otherwise, I think fashion
is useless.

Miuccia Prada

Referring to fashion as a projection of one's world vision,
vogue.com, February 12, 2024

The fluid lines and contemporary shapes of Prada's designs provided a template from which Miuccia was able to introduce more esoteric concepts to the Prada collections, often reasserting the political views that she once thought to be so at odds with the world of fashion.

But for me the goal is to be sexy in a different way, and that is not so easy. To be honest, what interests me more and more is the idea of what is real and what is unreal. What is beauty and what is fake? I'm wondering if we even can tell anymore.

Miuccia Prada

Challenging the notion that fashion must be "sexy" to be attractive, newyorker.com, March 7, 2004

Women have more facets.
We are so much more complex.
We are lovers, mothers, workers.

Miuccia Prada

On the undeniable influence of second-wave feminism in her visionary work, anothermag.com, December 10, 2018

My true point of view in fashion is to go against the cliches of beauty and sexy.

Miuccia Prada

On chafing against the cliches of beauty, wmagazine.com, December 11, 2015

I'm always trying to do something that is… never to please men in the most banal way.

Miuccia Prada

On standing out among her contemporaries when designing for women's lives, vogue.com, July 21, 2023

"

Every day you become older;
every day you feel a little more
outdated. The new blood of
[Miuccia] Prada, [Tom] Ford
makes me run more… [You] use
the talent of other people to
grow yourself.

"

Gianni Versace

Speaking to the *Washington Post* in 1997, veteran designer Gianni
Versace acknowledged the rise of Prada as stiff competition
through the 1990s, *Versace Catwalk: The Complete Collections* by
Tim Blanks, 2021

In my mind, it's so connected, the fashion, the art, the culture, the politics.

Miuccia Prada

On the interconnection between fashion and the world, vanityfair.com, August 1, 2019

To have an idea of a woman as a beautiful silhouette – no! I try to respect women – I tend not to do bias dresses, super-sexy. I try to be creative in a way that can be worn, that can be useful.

Miuccia Prada

On creating designs that are often seen as the antithesis of "sexy" fashion, vogue.com, February 12, 2024

Why do I love fashion? Because it's a very personal affair, almost like an intimate tale. Everyone loves fashion because they want to look beautiful.

Miuccia Prada

On the personal relationships with fashion, wmagazine.com, December 11, 2015

[Prada] rode the wave of less ostentatious design by offering key pieces or 'basics'; however, the impeccably cut and tailored clothes in luxurious materials that came with high price tags were anything but basic.

Emmanuelle Dirix

High Fashion: The 20th Century Decade by Decade, 2015

It's not necessarily about being rich or expensive but you don't have to be banal; dressing and elegance is more complicated than that. You have to try and elevate the level of dressing in some way, make it more thought out.

Miuccia Prada

On the complexities of fashion, anothermag.com, December 10, 2018

Clothes were never about doing clothes. It's about living different parts of your personality.

Miuccia Prada

On how clothing reflects our personality, *New York Times Style Magazine*, October 22, 2023

The Spring/Summer 1996 collection was a true turning point for Prada.

Using eccentric, clashing patterns in dull colours that had not been in fashion since the 1970s, this groundbreaking collection gave rise to Prada's signature concept of "ugly chic".

Fashion never opened itself to the 'ugly'. I started it, and I have been criticized a lot for this. But that has been the success of Prada.

Miuccia Prada

On the response to the seminal Spring/Summer 1996 collection, wmagazine.com, December 11, 2015

The clothes Miuccia Prada makes aren't sanitized, or elegant, or even necessarily attractive. But they still create a desire. We don't like them, but we want them.

Alexander Fury

Fashion critic Alexander Fury on Prada's "ugly chic" aesthetic, "Miuccia Prada - The Master of 'Ugly'", showstudio.com, June 12, 2024

Dressing models, including Kate Moss, in deliberately "nerdy" and clunky clothes divided audiences and critics alike, cementing Miuccia's reputation, once again, as an intellectual and challenging designer.

When I do ugly things it's completely intentional. In the end, if you always do only what you like, it becomes boring, you don't grow, you don't learn anything new.

Miuccia Prada

On bucking trends with the 1996 "ugly chic" collection, anothermag.com, December 10, 2018

It's much cooler than being
eccentric. With Mrs Prada, it's that
thing of style with substance. It's
not just a shell that looks good.

Marc Jacobs

Legendary designer Marc Jacobs on Miuccia, *New York Times Style Magazine*, October 22, 2023

The problem is only to have enough great ideas to be able to interpret the world, to be forward-thinking, to create something new, interesting, to go to the next step.

Miuccia Prada

On her creative process, vanityfair.com, August 1, 2019

Of course badness is everywhere – in the movies, in art, in life, but somehow what they call *bad taste* was never accepted in fashion. Back then it was kind of a scandal, an insult; even now, fashion is sometimes the place of clichéd beauty, but it's the cliché of beauty that has to be completely taken away – yes, changed.

Miuccia Prada

On bad taste vs ugly chic, vogue.com, February 12, 2024

Miuccia is trying to keep up with the zeitgeist. The danger for her in fashion is that if she is too experimental she will lose her clients. With art, she can try new things. But in the end it all fits together: art, fashion, architecture, design – even shopping. It's all theatre, really. A modern spectacle for a modern world.

Germano Celant

Italian art historian and critic, newyorker.com, March 7, 2004

TOP TEN

Throughout her career, Miuccia Prada has maintained that fashion is just one part of the larger culture conversation, and that different aspects of fashion can reflect different facets of individuality.

Spring/Summer 1988

Miuccia Prada's debut ready-to-wear collection introduced a minimalist aesthetic that challenged the flamboyant trends of the 1980s.

It set the tone for Prada's future, emphasizing clean lines and understated elegance.

Spring/Summer 1996

Known as the "Bad Taste" collection, it included clashing patterns and offbeat accessories, establishing Prada's reputation for intellectual and avant-garde fashion.

Fall/Winter 1998

This collection is famous for its severe aesthetic.

It featured dark, muted colours and minimalist designs, solidifying Prada's status as a leader in the "ugly chic" space.

Spring/Summer 2000

This sporty, futuristic collection showcased Prada's ability to blend luxury with functionality, paving the way for athleisure trends.

Spring/Summer 2004

Noted for its use of bold, graphic prints and vibrant colours, this collection reflected a more playful, artistic side of Prada.

Fall/Winter 2008

Featuring austere, military-inspired looks with rich textures and intricate detailing, this collection underscored Prada's knack for combining historical references with modern design.

Spring/Summer 2011

Also known as the "banana" collection, SS11 was a riot of colour and pattern, inspired by Latin American culture and showcasing Prada's talent for creating visually striking, culturally infused garments.

Fall/Winter 2012

Returning to the 1960s for inspiration, geometric patterns and vintage silhouettes were featured across both the womenswear and menswear collection.

Spring/Summer 2014

Possibly Prada's most overtly feminist collection, featuring bold, colourful designs, blending art and social commentary.

#10

Fall/Winter 2020

This was Prada's first collection to use recycled fabrics and eco-friendly production techniques, notably the recycled polyester known as Extreme-Text, developed exclusively for Prada.

I am interested in the lives of people. So, it's not *designing* – it's putting together personalities, histories, pieces of life, good, bad.

Miuccia Prada

On the complexities of designing, vogue.com, February 12, 2024

Honouring her
belief that fashion is
multifaceted,
Miuccia Prada opened
a second fashion
line in 1993:

Miu Miu.

I personally have many characters in myself and I think that many people have different characters in themselves: the feminine part and the masculine part, the gentle and the tough.

Miuccia Prada

On the complexities of the human character, vogue.com, February 12, 2024

Decent is not enough.

Miuccia Prada

On perfectionism, vogue.com, February 12, 2024

Fashion is a little small thing, I think:
Get dressed in the morning, and
afterwards you do something else.

Miuccia Prada

On fashion being the least important part of the day,
thatsnotmyage.com, February 12, 2024

I want culture to be attractive.

Miuccia Prada

Hoping for changes in fashion trends, vogue.com,
February 12, 2024

Named after her childhood pet name, Miu Miu was directed at a younger customer, with more youthful, vibrant and colourful designs.

Miu Miu is often called "Prada's little sister".

It's about the bad girls I knew at school, the ones I envied.

Miuccia Prada

On the inspiration behind Miu Miu, *The Little Book of Prada*, 2012

Something that has become old-fashioned is this obsession with youth, it's boring! And the idea to dress only comfortably, what does it mean? Who cares? Things can also be complicated, as life is.

Miuccia Prada

On society's emphasis on youth, anothermag.com, December 10, 2018

When people say, 'Are you happy about your achievement in fashion?' I really, sincerely, couldn't care less. I think about what I have to do next. I am ambitious, I want to be good. And sometimes I think I am good – a great exhibition, a good piece of clothing – but only for a second.

Miuccia Prada

Earning her reputation as a "powerhouse" in fashion, vogue.com, February 12, 2024

When they ask me how I can be elegant, well dressed – I say study! Study fashion, study movies, study art and after that study yourself.

Miuccia Prada

On her secret to elegance, anothermag.com, December 10, 2018

CHAPTER
FOUR

ART & INNOVATION

PRADA'S COMMITMENT TO
INNOVATION AND CONTEMPORARY
CULTURE EXTENDS BEYOND THE
END OF THE RUNWAY.

WHETHER THAT'S ART, BEAUTY,
SPORTSWEAR, MENSWEAR OR
EVEN THE SHOPPING EXPERIENCE
ITSELF, PRADA ALWAYS BRINGS
THAT UNIQUE BLEND OF
CURIOSITY AND CREATIVITY TO
EVERY NEW SPACE.

I would have been bored only doing bags.

Miuccia Prada

On the expansion of her empire, newyorker.com, March 7, 2004

Ever the innovator,
Prada has expanded from
bags and shoes into fashion,
menswear, streetwear,
beauty and even into art and
architecture.

[I hope I have not] thrown my life out on superficial things.

Miuccia Prada

Referencing a fear that fashion is ultimately superficial, *New York Times Style Magazine*, October 22, 2023

I never liked my work in theory,
but I loved it in practice.

Miuccia Prada

On loving her day-to-day work, newyorker.com, March 7, 2004

In 1992, Prada launched
its first menswear collection,
making it one of the first
fashion houses to do so.

Showing the same attention
to structure and design, the
Prada Man collection debuted
with a mixture of textiles
and fluid shapes.

When I design menswear, I try to identify myself as a man, and what I would like to wear as a man.

Miuccia Prada

On understanding the mindset and fashion choices of a man, wmagazine.com, December 11, 2015

"

This eccentricity and experimental approach to design, where modern and traditional techniques were fused together, resulted in a new perspective. Customers were now offered a delicate balance between classic and modern, whichattracted creatives and fashionistas, as well as intellectuals.

"

Laia Farran Graves

The Little Book of Prada, Carlton Books, 2012

Fashion is instant language.

One of Miuccia Prada's most influential quotes,
harpersbazzaar.com, February 3, 2022

Prada plays with the traditional concepts of masculinity and femininity, often choosing male models who are not considered traditionally good-looking.

They broke the mould again in the Fall/Winter 2024 menswear collection by scrapping models altogether in favour of actors who are often cast in a "villain role", including Willem Dafoe, Tim Roth, Adrien Brody, Gary Oldman, Emile Hirsch, Garrett Hedlund and Jamie Bell.

I leave it to other people to say what I did.

Miuccia Prada

Her humble take on her legacy of unconventional thinking and fashion-forward ideas, *New York Times Style Magazine*, October 22, 2023

Continuing to expand the Prada-verse, the first Prada cosmetics were launched in 2000 with Prada Beauty.

These were quickly followed in 2004 with Prada's first fragrances for men and women.

Prada Amber, created by Max and Clement Gavarry in collaboration with Carlos Benaim, is now considered a modern classic, with top notes of bergamot, orange, rose and patchouli.

Maybe due to the fact that it was created by a female hand, the fragrance is not aggressive at all, like it might have been expected from an oriental fragrance with leather and amber. Instead, it is very elegant and masculine gentle.

Miuccia Prada

On creating the first Prada Amber *Pour Homme* scent, glamobserver.com, April 11, 2024

While some may liken fashion to art, Miuccia Prada's involvement with the art world does not end at the bottom of a catwalk.

In 1993, Miuccia Prada and Patrizio Bertelli set up a non-profit foundation called Prada Milano Arte, focusing on contemporary sculpture.

The language of fashion is spontaneous and all of it has to do with art: you cannot actually make fashion if you do not have the desire to go outside the lines.

Miuccia Prada

On the relationship between fashion and art, *Italy Segreta*, January 2022

When they say you are sponsoring culture, I say, 'No – we want to be part of creating culture.' It's not about money – it's about bringing together efforts, people; proposing and finding solutions.

Miuccia Prada

On her passion for supporting artistic endeavours, vogue.com, February 12, 2024

I was never interested in art. My cultural background is based on movies, dance, theatre and books. Never visual arts... Collecting art is a learning process. And I like to work with artists.

Miuccia Prada

On her journey from theatre to art connoisseur, wmagazine.com, December 11, 2015

I laugh when they talk about fashion as art. It's ridiculous. When I buy art, I want to keep it separate. You don't want people to think you are doing what you are doing because you want to make your company better.

Miuccia Prada

On separating her work life from her creative life, newyorker.com, March 7, 2004

I didn't want, for any reason, people to think that I wanted to take advantage of the art to make my work more glamorous. Maybe I'm the last professional moralist.

Miuccia Prada

Reflecting on the relationship between fashion and art, vanityfair.com, August 1, 2019

Prada Marfa

Prada's most ambitious sculpture was also one of its most controversial: *Prada Marfa*, a permanent sculptural art installation by Scandinavian artists Elmgreen & Dragset.

The work was a freestanding building mimicking a typical Prada storefront, set on a barren stretch of road in Texas.

Made with biodegradable materials, the fake store was originally conceived as a commentary on gentrification and neoliberalism.

Stocked with donated Prada bags and shoes, the goal of the building was for it to slowly decay back into the landscape.

The site attracted vandals right away, as well as graffiti and local protestors.

Eventually the plan to let the sculpture slowly degrade was also scrapped, owing to health-and-safety concerns.

"

When people interact with
[public art], even vandalism can
be seen as a positive – it's a sign
of people feeling that they have
a say in public space.

"

Michael Elmgreen

One half of Elmgreen & Dragset, the sculptors of Prada Marfa,
theguardian.com, October 3, 2019

Prada Marfa cemented its place in culture through increased social media interest, a visit by Beyoncé and even a mention on *The Simpsons.*

After all these years, you come out here and the landscape, the collection, the way the bags are standing, is exactly the same. Nothing is ever like that.

Ingar Dragset

The other half of Elmgreen & Dragset, theguardian.com, October 3, 2019

Shopping Revolution

Uninspired with
shopping experiences,
Prada developed two
types of store:
the traditional "Green"
store (characterized by the
signature pale green walls)
and high-tech
Prada Epicentres.

Despite rumours of a fraught relationship, Dutch architect Rem Koolhaas designed both the first Prada Epicentre in New York and the second in Rodeo Drive, Los Angeles.

66

I tried to inject instability to make a radical space. You never know what you are going to get here.

99

Rem Koolhaas

Provocative Dutch architect Rem Koolhaas was commissioned to build the first Prada Epicentre in New York, anothermag.com, May 3, 2018

It couldn't just be a nice display for objects and clothes but not make any statement about architecture. It had to be a place for special events, and to address the problem of a company becoming big and wanting to stay small and sophisticated – all the contradictions that come with wanting to grow.

Miuccia Prada

On the paradoxes of the Prada Epicentres, latimes.com,
July 14, 2004

Today, there are three
Prada Epicentres:
New York, Los Angeles
and Tokyo.

Making its mark with
bags, shoes, clothes, beauty,
menswear and even art
and architecture, Prada
truly is a cultural force to
be reckoned with.

Of course, anytime you go somewhere, you learn something.

Miuccia Prada

On her life-long learning journey, vanityfair.com, August 1, 2019

CHAPTER
FIVE

THEATRE & FILM

OFTEN NOTED AS ONE OF THE
FIRST FASHION HOUSES TO BRING
ELEMENTS OF PERFORMANCE ART
AND FILM INTO THEIR SHOWS,
PRADA'S INFLUENCE EXTENDS OUT
INTO THE WORLD OF THEATRE
AND MOVIES. OF COURSE,
THAT'S EVEN BEFORE MENTIONING
THE DEVIL WEARS PRADA...

Owing to Miuccia Prada's own personal history with the theatre, it is no surprise that Prada's designs have made it onto stage and screen.

"

Sometimes she's a little bit ahead of the curve, and the curve has to catch up. Miuccia has such a knack, not for what is popular right now, but for what will be popular even years down the road.

"

Baz Luhrmann

Long-time collaborator and legendary filmmaker, vanityfair.com, August 1, 2019

Baz Luhrmann and Miuccia Prada have been long-time friends and collaborators. Their work together began on Luhrmann's iconic 1996 adaptation, *Romeo + Juliet*.

66

25 years on, *Romeo + Juliet*'s costume design shines as an exemplary example of style and substance. It aids Luhrmann's postmodern, hyper-colourful world by being just as colourful and unique whilst adding a new layer of depth to the characters and storytelling.

99

Prada's designs were central to the iconic look of the 1996 movie, newwavemag.com

As well as designing Juliet's (played by Claire Danes) show-stopping white angel wings, Prada also designed a bespoke blue wedding suit for Romeo (played by Leonardo DiCaprio).

However, Prada's next foray into film would be just as iconic, if albeit a reluctant one: the 2006 adaptation of Lauren Weisberger's 2003 bestselling book, *The Devil Wears Prada*.

"

Florals? For Spring?
Groundbreaking.

"

Miranda Priestly

Played by Meryl Streep, as the titular "Devil" in Prada,
graziamagazine.com, June 22, 2021

I was terrified: the book was awful. The film, on the other hand, was fun.

Miuccia Prada

Taking the success of *The Devil Wears Prada* in her stride, hellomagazine.com, April 29, 2015

Loosely based on *Vogue*'s Anna Wintour, Miranda Priestly, the boss of the fictional *Runway* magazine, is played by Meryl Streep, whose wardrobe in the film is in fact about 40% Prada, according to the custome designer Patricia Field.

For a while it seemed that that association was the only flattering thing about the enterprise, and Miuccia and I never discussed it. Finally, at one of our lunches, she leaned across the table and she said, 'Anna, that book, it's good for both of us.' And the subject has never come up again.

Anna Wintour

Said to be the inspiration for the character of Miranda Priestly, the *Vogue* editor-in-chief addresses how the movie impacted both herself and Miuccia Prada, refinery29.com, November 16, 2016

In a nod to the film's title, Anna Wintour attended the opening night of *The Devil Wears Prada* wearing Prada.

> 66
>
> I own one pair of Prada shoes.
> They make my feet hurt… It's not
> the shoes' fault; they are exquisitely
> made. I blame my feet. I've got my
> mother's feet.
>
> 99

Meryl Streep

On the truth behind her Prada wardrobe, nzherald.co.nz,
September 26, 2006

Prada's next foray into film
was another unexpected twist.

Interestingly, Miuccia's
first film credit is for costume
consulting on the 2007
Japanese science-fiction
animated film,
Appleseed: Ex Machina.

However, returning to her more comfortable theatrical roots, Miuccia Prada designed the costumes for Giuseppe Verdi's opera *Attila*, which premiered in New York's Metropolitan Opera in 2010.

"

There's a difference between like and love. Because I like my Skechers, but I love my Prada backpack.

Bianca

Played by Larisa Oleynik, in the 1999 classic movie *10 Things I Hate About You*, *New York Times Style Magazine*, October 22, 2023

A fashion show is kind of a movie.

Miuccia Prada

On the crossover between fashion and film, wmagazine.com,
September 5, 2018

It's the toughest industry to work in. But you know what has made me appreciate my job? The super-clever people around me – directors, artists and intellectuals who appreciate the ideas. I have always believed in collaborations and made sure I worked with and supported female artists.

Miuccia Prada

Talking to Cate Blanchett about the crossover between theatre and fashion, wmagazine.com, September 5, 2018

66

You quickly sense her vulnerability, which can sort of disappear from a person with such authority. I think without a bit of that, you can't quite reach them. She can be fearless, but I don't think she's fearless.

99

Wes Anderson

The movie director on Miuccia Prada's character, *New York Times Style Magazine*, October 22, 2023

Prada returned to a collaboration with Baz Luhrmann and his wife and costume designer Catherine Martin in the opulent 2013 adaption of *The Great Gatsby.*

Miuccia said to me, 'I don't think
I ever think about the 20s. I only think
about periods that I've lived or have
had an association with through my
family – the 40s, 50s, 60s, 70s'. But
she was interested in the collaboration
because she liked the idea that there
were these subconscious themes that
have been coming out of her work.

Catherine Martin

On how Prada's designs "accidentally" worked perfectly with the
1920s costume design of *The Great Gatsby*, collectorsweekly.com,
September 18, 2013

That's what's interesting. The point of view can transform things so much. Yes, probably a few [dresses] had that kind of edge, but almost none were meant to be the 20s when I did them. I was really fascinated by that.

Miuccia Prada

On how her designs had been "accidentally" reminiscent of the 1920s and subsequently perfect for *The Great Gatsby*, wwd.com, April 30, 2013

Baz and Miuccia have always connected on their shared fascination with finding modern ways of releasing classic and historical references from the shackles of the past.

Catherine Martin

The costume designer discusses the relationship between Baz Luhrmann and Miuccia Prada, vogue.co.uk, January 21, 2013

Martin and Prada achieved *The Great Gatsby*'s modernized 1920s look by altering pieces from Prada's and Miu Miu's archives, many of which had not at the time made it off the catwalk.

Once again, Prada, Martin and Luhrmann sought to re-imagine historical fashion with a contemporary twist in 2023's *Elvis*, starring Austin Butler and Tom Hanks.

It was wonderful for both Baz
and me to creatively collaborate
with Miuccia once again. By
immersing ourselves in the Prada
and Miu Miu archives with highly
trained workshops, we brought
the Presleys' historic clothing into
the wardrobe that would be in
the film.

Catherine Martin

On the costume design used in the film *Elvis*, graziamagazine.com.

In 2004, Miuccia Prada was awarded the Council of Fashion Designers of America International Award.

In 2015, for her contribution to fashion, Miuccia was awarded Knight of the Grand Cross, the highest honorary title of the Order of Merit of the Italian Republic.

Basically, now every fashion house is a cultural platform. But Prada did it 30 years ago.

Francesco Vezzoli

Italian artist and close friend of Miuccia, Francesco Vezzoli, *New York Times Style Magazine,* October 22, 2023

Someone once asked me, 'Why art? Why fashion?' and I said, 'Because they are my instruments.' If I were a doctor, I would use the available science. They are instruments of knowledge used to make ideas available.

Miuccia Prada

On the "instruments" of her creativity, anothermag.com, December 10, 2018

Prada
SHORT MOVIES

As well as designing costumes for film and stage, Prada was one of the first fashion houses to produce its own short artistic films to coincide with the concepts of its new seasons.

Thunder Perfect Mind
(February 2005)

Trembled Blossoms
(February 2008)

Fallen Shadows
(September 2008)

Alchemy
(October 2008)

First Spring
(January 2010)

A Therapy
(May 2012)

Prada Candy L'Eau
(April 2013)

Castello Cavalcanti
(November 2013)

Past Forward
(November 2016)

Your main obligation is to yourself. We are our own best competitors.

Miuccia Prada

Words of wisdom from the icon herself, wmagazine.com, September 5, 2018